Lyman Copeland Draper

Narrative of a journey down the Ohio and Mississippi in

1789-90

Lyman Copeland Draper

Narrative of a journey down the Ohio and Mississippi in 1789-90

ISBN/EAN: 9783337128159

Printed in Europe, USA, Canada, Australia, Japan

Cover: Foto ©Andreas Hilbeck / pixelio.de

More available books at **www.hansebooks.com**

Lyman Copeland Draper

Narrative of a journey down the Ohio and Mississippi in 1789-90

ISBN/EAN: 9783337128159

Printed in Europe, USA, Canada, Australia, Japan

Cover: Foto ©Andreas Hilbeck / pixelio.de

More available books at **www.hansebooks.com**

NARRATIVE

OF A

JOURNEY

DOWN THE OHIO AND MISSISSIPPI

IN 1789-90.

BY
MAJ. SAMUEL S. FORMAN

WITH A MEMOIR AND ILLUSTRATIVE NOTES

BY
LYMAN C. DRAPER

CINCINNATI
ROBERT CLARKE & CO
1888

NARRATIVE

OF A

JOURNEY

DOWN THE OHIO AND MISSISSIPPI

IN 1789-90.

BY
MAJ. SAMUEL S. FORMAN

WITH A MEMOIR AND ILLUSTRATIVE NOTES

BY
LYMAN C. DRAPER

CINCINNATI
ROBERT CLARKE & CO
1888

PREFATORY NOTE.

I ACKNOWLEDGE my indebtedness to a friend of the Forman family for calling my attention to the interesting narrative of Major Samuel S. Forman's early journey down the Ohio and Mississippi, and for aiding me in securing a copy for publication. The manuscript of this monograph, as now presented, has been submitted to friends and kindred of Major Forman, who knew him long and well, and they have accorded it their warm approval.

With their kind approbation, I feel encouraged to offer this little contribution to western historical literature to an enlightened public. L. C. D.

MADISON, WIS.

MEMOIR

OF

MAJOR SAMUEL S. FORMAN.

EVERY addition to our stock of information touching early western history and adventure, and of the pioneer customs and habits of a hundred years ago, deserves a kindly reception. The following narrative of a journey down the Ohio and Mississippi, in 1789–90, was not reduced to writing till 1849, after a lapse of sixty years; but an unusually fine memory enabled Major Forman to relate such incidents of his trip as left a lasting impression upon him, alike with interest and general accuracy. A sketch of the writer will give us a better insight into his trustworthiness and character.

Major Forman, the third son of Samuel and Helena Denise Forman, was born at Middletown Point, Monmouth county, New Jersey, July 21, 1765. He was too young to participate in the Revolutionary war, during the stirring period of 1776 to 1780, in New Jersey; but his elder brothers, Jonathan and Denise, were prominent and active throughout the great struggle. Major Forman has recorded some incidents of the war that occurred in his region of New Jersey, and within his own knowledge, worthy of preservation as interesting scraps of Revolutionary history. At one time, a cousin of his, Tunis Forman, about seventeen years of age, met two Tory robbers, and after one had fired at him and missed, he, getting the advantage of them in the adjustment of his gun, forced them to throw down their weapons, when he marched them several miles before him, and lodged them in jail at Freehold. For this brave act, young Forman received a large reward.*

During the period while Major Henry Lee and his famous Light Dragoons were serving in New Jersey, intelligence came of the marauding operations of a band of Tory robbers, located in the extensive pine woods toward Barnegat, in Monmouth county, whose head-quarters were at a secret cave in that region. Lee dispatched a select party of fearless men, who approached the dangerous region in a farmer's wagon, concealed under a covering of straw. Fagans, the robber leader, with some followers, stopped the wagon to plunder it, when the concealed dragoons immediately put a ball through Fagans's head, and with his fall his associates fled. Fagans's body was conveyed to Barkalow's woods, the usual place of execution for such culprits, and there exposed on a gibbet till the flesh dropped from the bones.

Mr. Forman mentions that his father, Samuel Forman, did not escape a visit from the Tories and British. At one time, they made a descent upon the village of Middletown Point. There was a mill at this place, which was well known and much resorted to for a great distance;

---

* This incident, occurring in May, 1780, is related in Barber and Howe's *New Jersey Historical Collection*, 345-6.

and some of these Tory invaders had been employed in the erection of this mill, and were personally well known to the citizens, and it would appear that their object was, at least, to capture Samuel Forman, if not to kill him. They plundered the houses of the settlement, destroying what they could not carry off, boasting that they had aided in building the mill, and now assisted in kindling the fire in the bolting box to burn it down. They had surprised the guard placed for the protection of the place, killing several of their number, who had been their schoolmates in former years. Samuel Forman eluded their vigilance, but lost heavily by this invasion, for he owned almost all of one side of Middletown Point, and part of both sides of Main street. He never applied to Congress for any remuneration for his losses. He died in 1792, in his seventy-eighth year. In this foray, the enemy burned two store-houses of Mr. John H. Burrows, robbed his house, and took him prisoner to New York. After several months, he was exchanged, and returned home.

My brother, Denise Forman, entered the service when he was about sixteen years old. He was in the battle of Germantown—in which engagement eighteen of the Forman connection took part—where the Americans were badly used, on account of the British having some light artillery in a large stone house. Our army had to retreat; when that took place, Lieutenant Schenck, under whom brother Denise served, took Denise's gun, and told him to take fast hold of his coat, and cling to it during the retreat. General David Forman conducted himself so well, that General Washington tendered his aid in securing a command in the Continental army; but General Forman declined the offer, as he believed he could be more serviceable to remain with the militia in Monmouth county, New Jersey, as they were continually harassed there by the enemy from Staten Island and New York.

After this, Denise Forman engaged under a Captain Tyler, who had charge of a few gun-boats that coasted along the Jersey shore, to annoy and oppose the enemy. When the British fleet lay at anchor near Sandy Hook, Captain Tyler went, in the night, and surprised a large sloop at anchor among the men-of-war. Tyler's party boarded the sloop, secured the sailors, weighed anchor, and got her out from the fleet, and took her up Middletown creek, all without any fighting. The whole enterprise was conducted with so much judgment, that the sailor prisoners dared not speak or give the least sign of alarm. "When we first touched the sloop," said Denise Forman," I felt for a moment a little streaked, but it was soon over, and then we worked fearlessly to get the vessel under weigh, without alarming the fleet." These gun-boats were all propelled by muffled oars, that dipped in and out of the water so as to make no noise; nor did any of the men speak above their breath. On the gunwale of the boat, a strip of heavy canvas was nailed, the inner edge having been left unfastened, under which were concealed their swords, guns, and other implements for use in a combat, and so placed that each man could, at an instant's notice, lay his hand upon his own weapon. Even in port, the men belonging to Tyler's party were not allowed to talk or speak to other people, as a matter of precaution; and the captain always spoke in an undertone, and if a man laid down an oar, it was always done as noiselessly as possible.

At one time, fifteen hundred British and Tories landed on Middletown shore, and marched from six to ten miles back into the country. A beacon, placed on a conspicuous hill, was fired for the purpose of giving an alarm; and soon the militia of the country, understanding the notice, gathered, and opposed the enemy. In Pleasant Valley they checked their advance. Uncle John Schenck and brother Denise so closely cornered a British or Tory officer of this party in a barn-yard, that he jumped from his horse, took to his heels and escaped, leaving his horse behind him.

Major Burrows* happened to be at home at that time, on a visit to his family. Some of the Americans dressed themselves in British red coats, which had been captured. The Rev. Mr. DuBois, who, like a good patriot, had turned out on this occasion, with his fowling-piece,

---

* Major John Burrows was first a captain in Colonel David Forman's regiment. Forman had the nick-name of "Black David," to distinguish him from a relative of the same name, and he was always a terror to the Tories; and Captain Burrows, from his efficiency against these marauders, was called by those enemies of the country, "Black David's Devil." January 1, 1777, Captain Burrows was made a captain in Spencer's regiment on Continental establishment; and, January 22, 1779, he was promoted to the rank of major, serving in Sullivan's campaign against the hostile Six Nations, and remaining in the army till the close of the war. Several years after, he went on a journey to the interior of Georgia, in an unhealthy season, when he probably sickened and died, for he was never heard of afterward.

Major Burrows left an interesting journal of Sullivan's campaign, which appears in the splendid volume on that campaign issued by the State of New York, in 1887. The original MS. journal is preserved by his grand-daughter, Mrs. Elizabeth Breese Stevens, of Sconondoa, Oneida county, New York.

when Major Burrows rode near by, eked out in British uniform; Mr. DuBois spoke to Captain Schenck, his brother-in-law, "Look, there is a good shot," and, suiting the action to the word, took deliberate aim. Captain Schenck, better understanding the situation, quickly knocked up the clergyman's gun, with the explanation— "Don't shoot; that's Major Burrows." Mr. DuBois supposed he was aiming at a British officer, within point blank shot, who was endeavoring to rejoin his fellows.

Denise Forman's next move was to enlist with Captain Philip Freneau, the well-known poet, who sailed from Philadelphia in a letter of marque, the *Aurora*, against British commerce on the high seas. While not long out, sailing toward the West Indies, Freneau and his adventurous vessel were captured by their enemies, sent to New York, and all incarcerated on board of the *Scorpion*, one of the prison ships floating in New York harbor and Wallabout Bay, its unhappy prisoners experiencing almost untold horrors. Captain Freneau, at least, was subsequently transferred to what he denominated "the loathsome *Hunter*." These prison ships attained an unenviable reputation for maltreating and half-starving their hapless and ill-fated victims, hundreds of whom died in consequence of their inhuman treatment. This sad experience became the subject of one of Freneau's subsequent poems, emanating from the depths of his embittered soul recollections. Brother Denise used to relate to me, after his return home, that, when on the prison ship, he had to shut his eyes whenever he ate the sea-biscuit or drank the water assigned him, so full were they of vermin! Freneau, in his poem, thus alludes to the fare with which the poor prisoners were treated:

"See, captain, see! what rotten bones we pick.
 What kills the healthy can not cure the sick.
 Not dogs on *such* by Christian men are fed;
 And see, good master, see that lousy bread!"

"Your meat or bread," this man of flint replied,
"Is not my care to manage or provide;
 But this, damn'd rebel dogs, I'd have you know,
 That better than you merit we bestow.
 Out of my sight!" No more he deigned to say,
 But whisk'd about, and, frowning, strode away.

When the survivors were exchanged, after their long imprisonment, they were so weak and emaciated that they could scarcely walk—perfect living skeletons; and my brother, after his return home, was confined to his bed, and for several days nearly all hope of his recovery was abandoned; but he at length providentially recovered. Denise Forman received a captain's commission when a war was threatened with France, in 1798, and when the army was disbanded, he settled on a farm in Freehold, where he spent the remainder of his days.

About 1790, Captain Freneau married my sister Eleanor. He was a prominent Anti-Federalist in his day, and edited various Democratic papers at different places, and was for a time translating clerk in the State Department. While he was able to translate the French documents, he found it cost him more than he received to get those in other foreign languages properly translated, and after a while he resigned. He had in early life been a college-mate with James Madison, at Princeton, and has been aptly called the "patriot poet" of the Revolution, his effusions having been useful to the cause of the country during its great struggle for independence.

He lost his life in a violent snow-storm, in December, 1832, in his eighty-first year, near Monmouth, New Jersey.

While attending grammar-school, the latter part of the Revolutionary war, at Freehold, young Forman records: The hottest part of the battle of Monmouth was about this spot, where my brother-in-law, Major Burrows, lived after he left the army, and with whom I and some fellow-students boarded. Our path to the school-house crossed a grave where a remarkably tall British officer was buried. We opened the grave; a few pieces only of blanket, which encompassed the corpse, remained. One school-mate, Barnes Smock, was a very tall person, but the thigh bones of this unfortunate officer far outmeasured his. I believe this was the only engagement when the two opposing armies had recourse to the bayonet,* and this was the place of that charge. The battle took place on the Sabbath. A British cannon ball went through Rev. Dr. Woodhull's church. Dr. Woodhull was now one of my teachers. The two armies lay upon their arms all night after the battle. General Washington and General La Fayette slept in their cloaks under an apple-tree in Mr. Henry Perrine's orchard. It was Washington's intention to have renewed the battle the next day, but the British, in the course of the night, stole a march as fast as they could for their fleet at Sandy Hook.

In the spring of 1783, when peace was dawning, many of the old citizens of New York City, who had been exiled from their homes for some seven years, began to re-

---

* This is an error. Bayonet charges were resorted to by Morgan at the Cowpens, and in other engagements.

turn to their abandoned domiciles, even before the British evacuation. Among them was Major Benjamin Ledyard, who had married my oldest sister. In September of that year, at the instance of my sister Ledyard, I went to New York as a member of her family. Every day I saw the British soldiers. Indeed, a young lieutenant boarded a short time in our family, as many families received the British officers as an act of courtesy.

Even before the British evacuation, the American officers were permitted to cross over into the city, and frequently came, visiting the coffee-houses and other places of public resort. Here they would meet British officers, and some of them evinced a strong inclination to make disturbance with their late competitors, throwing out hints or casting reflections well calculated to provoke personal combats. There was a Captain Stakes, of the American Light Dragoons, a fine, large, well-built man, who had no fear about him. It was said, when he entered the coffee-house, that the British officers exercised a wholesome caution how they treated him, after some of them had made a feint in testing his powers. But it all happily passed over without harm.

It was finally agreed between General Washington and Sir Guy Carleton that New York should be evacuated November 25th. In the morning of that day, the British army paraded in the Bowery. The Americans also paraded, and marched down till they came very close to each other, so that the officers of both armies held friendly parleys. The streets were crowded with people on an occasion so interesting. I hurried by the red-coats till I reached the Americans, where I knew I would be safe. So I sauntered about among the officers. Presently, an American officer seized me by the hand, when, I looking up at him, he said, encouragingly: "Don't be afraid, Sammy. I know your brother Jonathan. He is an officer in the same line with me, and my name is Cumming."* He continued to hold me by the hand till orders were given to advance. He advised me to keep on the sidewalk, as I might get run over in the street.

The British steadily marched in the direction of their vessels, while the Americans advanced down Queen (since Pearl) street; the British embarking on board their fleet on East river, I believe, near Whitehall, and the Americans headed directly to Fort George, on the point where the Battery now is. Stockades were around the fort, and the large gate was opened. When the British evacuated the fort, they unreefed the halyards of the tall flagstaff, greased the pole, so that it was some time before the American flag was hoisted. At length, a young soldier† succeeded in climbing the pole, properly arranged the halyards, when up ran the striped and star-spangled banner, amid the deafening shouts of the multitude, that

---

* This was John N. Cumming, who rose from a lieutenant to be lieutenant-colonel, commanding the Third New Jersey Regiment, serving the entire war.

† The editor, while at Saratoga Springs, in 1838, took occasion to visit the venerable Anthony Glean, who resided in the town of Saratoga, and who was reputed to be the person who climbed the greased flag-staff at the evacuation of New York, and who himself claimed to have performed that feat. He was then a well-to-do farmer, enjoying a pension for his revolutionary services, and lived two or three years later, till he had reached the age of well-nigh ninety. The newspapers of that period often referred to him as the hero of the flag-staff exploit, and no one called it in question.

seemed to shake the city. It is easier to imagine than to describe the rejoicing, and the brilliancy of the fireworks that evening.

After the evacuation, Mr. Forman witnessed the affectionate and affecting parting of Washington and his officers, when he entered a barge at Whitehall wharf, manned by sea captains in white frocks, who rowed him to the Jersey shore, to take the stage for Philadelphia, on his way to Congress. Mr. Forman also saw General Washington while presiding over the convention of 1787, to form a Constitution for the new Republic. The general was attired in citizen's dress—blue coat, cocked hat, hair in queue, crossed and powdered. He walked alone to the State House, the place of meeting, and seemed pressed down in thought. A few moments before General Washington took his seat on the rostrum, the venerable Dr. Franklin, one of the Pennsylvania delegates, was brought in by a posse of men in his sedan, and helped into the hall, he being severely afflicted with palsy or paralysis at the time. On the adoption of the Constitution, a great celebration was held in New York to commemorate the event, which Mr. Forman also witnessed. A large procession was formed, composed of men of all avocations in life, and each represented by some insignia of his own trade or profession, marching through the streets with banners, flags, and stirring music. A full-rigged vessel, called "The Federal Ship Hamilton," was drawn in the procession, and located in Bowling Green, where it remained until it fell to pieces by age.

After spending some years as a clerk in mercantile establishments in New York City, and once going as supercargo to dispose of a load of flour to Charleston, he engaged in merchandising at Middletown Point, New Jersey. Mr. Forman subsequently made the journey down the Ohio and Mississippi, in 1789–'90, as given in considerable detail in the narrative which follows. While spending the winter of 1792–'93 in Philadelphia, he witnessed the inauguration of Washington as President, at the beginning of his second term of office, and was within six feet of him when he took the oath of office. "I cast my eyes over the vast crowd," says Major Forman, "and every eye seemed riveted on the great chief. On Washington's right sat Chief-Justice Cushing, and on his left Senator Langdon, of New Hampshire. After sitting a little while in profound silence, the senator arose, and asked the President if he was ready to take the oath of office. General Washington rose up, having a paper in his left hand, when he made a very short address. Then Judge Cushing stood up, with a large open Bible before him, facing the President, who laid his hand upon the sacred volume, and very deliberately and distinctly repeated the oath of office as pronounced by the chief-justice. When Washington repeated his own name, as he did at the conclusion of the ceremony, it made my blood run cold. The whole proceedings were performed with great solemnity. General Washington was dressed in deep mourning, for, it was said, a favorite nephew who had lived at Mount Vernon during the Revolutionary war. He wore his mourning sword. Mrs. Washington was about the middling stature, and pretty fleshy."

Mr. Forman now entered into the employ of the Holland Land Company, through their agents, Theophilus Cazenove and John Lincklaen, to found a settlement in the back part of the State of New York, where that company had purchased a large body of land. He accordingly headed a party, in conjunction with Mr. Lincklaen, for this purpose, conveying a load of merchandise to the point of operations, passing in batteaus up the Mohawk to old Fort Schuyler, now Utica, beyond which it was necessary to open up a road for the teams and loads of goods: lodging in the woods when necessary, living on raw pork and bread, which was better than the bill of fare at the well-known tavern in that region, kept by John Dennie, the half Indian—"no bread, no meat;" and one of Dennie's descendants indignantly resented being referred to as an Indian—"Me no Indian; only Frenchman and squaw!" At length, May 8, 1793, the party arrived on the beautiful body of water, since known as Cazenovia Lake, and founded the village of Cazenovia, where Mr. Forman engaged in felling trees, and erecting the necessary houses in which to live and do business, and in this rising settlement he engaged in merchandising for several years. He held many public positions of honor and trust; was county clerk, secretary for over thirty years of a turnpike company; served as major in a regiment of militia early organized at Cazenovia.

The latter years of his life he spent in Syracuse, where he was greatly respected for his worth, his fine conversational powers, his social and generous feelings. He lived to the great age of over ninety-seven years, dying August 16, 1862. His closing years were embittered over the distracted condition of his country, embroiled in fratricidal war, and his prayer was that the proud flag which he witnessed when it was placed over the ramparts of Fort George, November 25, 1783, might again wave its ample folds over a firmly united American Confederacy. His patriotic prayer was answered, though he did not himself live to witness it.

NARRATIVE OF A JOURNEY
DOWN THE OHIO AND MISSISSIPPI,

1789-'90.

GENERAL DAVID FORMAN,* of New Jersey, entered into a negotiation with the Spanish minister, Don Diego de Gardoque, for his brother, Ezekiel Forman, of Philadelphia, to emigrate with his family and sixty odd colored people, and settle in the Natchez country, then under Spanish authority.

I agreed with General Forman to accompany the emigrating party; and, about the last of November, 1789, having closed up my little business at Middletown Point, New Jersey, I set out from the general's residence, in Freehold, with Captain Benajah Osmun, an old continental captain, who was at that time the faithful overseer of the general's blacks. There were sixty men, women, and children, and they were the best set of blacks I

---

*General Forman was born near Englishtown, Monmouth Co., New Jersey. He was, during the Revolutionary war, a terror to the tories of his region, and as brigadier-general commanded the Jersey troops at the battle of Germantown. No less than eighteen of the Forman connection were in his brigade in this engagement. He was subsequently a county judge, and member of the council of state. He died about 1812.

ever saw together. I knew the most of them, and all were well-behaved, except two rather ill-tempered fellows. General Forman purchased some more, who had intermarried with his own, so as not to separate families. They were all well fed and well clothed.

We had, I believe, four teams of four horses each, and one two-horse wagon, all covered with tow-cloth, while Captain Osmun and I rode on horseback. After the distressing scene of taking leave—for the general's family and blacks were almost all in tears—we sat out upon our long journey. The first night we camped on the plains near Cranberry, having accomplished only about twelve or fifteen miles. The captain and I had a bed put under one of the wagons; the sides of the wagon had tenter-hooks, and curtains made to hook up to them, with loops to peg the bottom to the ground. The colored people mostly slept in their wagons. In the night a heavy rain fell, when the captain and I fared badly. The ground was level, and the water, unable to run off, gave us a good soaking. I had on a new pair of handsome buckskin small clothes; the rain spoiled their beauty, and the wetting and subsequent shrinkage rendered them very uncomfortable to wear.

The next morning we commenced our journey as early as possible. We drove to Princeton, where we tarried awhile, and all were made comfortable. We crossed the Delaware five miles above Trenton. On arriving at Lancaster, in Pennsylvania, the authorities stopped us, as we somewhat expected they would do. General Forman had furnished me with all the necessary papers relating to the transportation of slaves through New Jersey and Pennsylvania. While Judge Hubley was examining the papers, the servant women informed me that the females of the city came out of their houses and inquired of them whether they could spin, knit, sew, and do housework, and whether they were willing to go to the South; so, if the authorities stopped us, they could all soon have new homes. But our colored women laughed at the Lancaster ladies, who seemed mortified when they learned that we could not be detained.

In Westmoreland county we had a little trouble with a drunken justice of the peace and some free blacks These free blacks, as we learned from a faithful old colored woman, furnished the two ill-tempered blacks of our party with old swords and pistols, but nothing serious grew out of it.

The weather began to grow very cold, the roads bad, and traveling tedious. We encamped one night in the woods, kindled a fire, and turned the tails of the wagons all inward, thus forming a circle around the fire. Another night we came to a vacant cabin without a floor; we made a large fire, and all who chose took their bedding and slept in the cabin, some remaining in the wagons. The captain and I had our beds spread before the fire.

One Saturday evening, we were apprehensive of being obliged to encamp again in the woods. I went ahead, hoping to find night quarters. I rode up to a log house and went in; it was growing dark, and I began to ask the landlord to accommodate us for the night, addressing myself to a tall, lean man. Before I got through with my inquiry, he caught me up in his arms, as if I were merely a small child, and exclaimed: "Mighty souls! if this is not little Sammy Forman," and, hugging and kissing me, added, "Why, don't you remember Charley Morgan? Yes, you can have any thing I have, and we will do the best we can for you." This was somewhere in the Alleghany mountains, and here we remained till Monday, buying wheat, and sending it to mill, and converting a fat steer into meat, so that we were well provided for, for awhile. This Charley Morgan entered the regular service as a corporal in my brother Jonathan's company, when he was a captain, and raised his company in the vicinity of Middletown Point, New Jersey. He could ape the simpleton very well, and was sent as a spy into the British army, and returned safe with the desired information. I was surprised to meet him in this far-off mountain region.

Somewhere about Fort Littleton or Fort Loudon, our funds ran out. When we left General Forman, he told me that Uncle Ezekiel Forman would leave Philadelphia with his family, and overtake us in time to supply our wants. But he did not start as soon as he expected, and on his way in the mountains the top of his carriage got broken by a leaning tree, which somewhat detained him, so that we arrived at Pittsburg two or three days before him.

One morning, while in the neighborhood of Fort Littleton or Fort Loudon, I offered to sell my horse to the landlord where we took breakfast; he kept a store as well as a tavern, and was wealthy. The price of the horse I put very low, when the landlord asked why I offered him so cheap. I informed him that I was out of funds, and had expected that Ezekiel Forman, who owned the colored people, would have overtaken us before our means became exhausted. He replied: "I know your uncle, and I will lend you as much money as you need, and take your order on him, as he will stop here on his way. Now, step with me to the store." Pointing to the large piles of silver dollars on the counter in the store, he said: "Step up and help yourself to as much as you want, and give me your order." This was an unexpected favor. When uncle arrived, he satisfied the order.

It had taken us near three weeks to journey from Monmouth to Pittsburg. After our arrival at this place, our first business was to find situations for our numerous family, while awaiting the rise of the Ohio, and to lay in provisions for our long river voyage. Colonel Turnbull, late of Philadelphia, and an acquaintance of uncle, politely offered him the use of a vacant house and storeroom, exactly such apartments as were wanted. The colored people were all comfortably housed also.

The horses and wagons were sold at a great sacrifice—uncle retaining only his handsome coach horses and carriage, which he took to Natchez on a tobacco boat, which Captain Osmun commanded, and on board of which the colored field hands were conveyed. These boats were flat-bottomed, and boarded over the top, and appeared like floating houses. Uncle's boat was a seventy feet keel-boat, decked over, with a cabin for lodging purposes, but too low to stand up erect. The beds and bedding lay on the floor, and the insides lined with plank to prevent the Indians from penetrating through with their balls, should they attack us. We had a large quantity of dry goods, and a few were opened and bartered in payment for boats and provisions.

On board of the keel-boat, uncle and family found comfortable quarters. Mr. and Mrs. Forman, Augusta,

Margaret, and Frances, aged about nine, eleven, and thirteen, and David Forman and Miss Betsey Church, the latter housekeeper and companion for Aunt Forman, an excellent woman, who had lived in the family several years, and occasionally took the head of the table. I and five or six others, two mechanics, and about eight or ten house servants, were also occupants of this boat.

The family received much polite attention while in Pittsburg. By the time we got prepared for our departure, the Ohio river rose. We tarried there about a month. Both boats were armed with rifles, pistols, etc. It being in Indian war time, all boats descending that long river, of about eleven hundred miles, were liable to be attacked every hour by a merciless foe, oftentimes led on by renegade whites.

Uncle fixed on a certain Sabbath, as was the custom in those days, to embark on ship-board. On that day, the polite and hospitable Colonel Turnbull, then a widower, gave uncle an elegant dinner, and invited several gentlemen to grace the occasion with their presence. After dinner, which was not prolonged, we embarked on board our little squadron. Colonel Wm. Wyckoff, and his brother-in-law, Kenneth Scudder, of Monmouth county, New Jersey, accompanied us on our voyage. The colonel had been, seven years previous to this, an Indian trader, and was now on his way to Nashville, Tennessee.

Uncle Forman's keel-boat, Captain Osmun's flat-boat, and Colonel Wyckoff's small keel-boat constituted our little fleet. The day of our departure was remarkably pleasant. Our number altogether must have reached very nearly a hundred. The dinner party accompanied us to our boats, and the wharf was covered with citizens. The river was very high, and the current rapid. It was on the Monongahela where we embarked.

Our keel-boat took the lead. These boats are guided by oars, seldom used, except the steering oar, or when passing islands, as the current goes about six or seven miles an hour. As the waters were now high, the current was perhaps eight or nine miles an hour. Before day-break next morning we made a narrow escape from destruction, from our ignorance of river navigation. We had an anchor and cable attached to our keel-boat. The cable was made fast to small posts over the forecastle, where were fenders all around the little deck. When it began to grow dark, the anchor was thrown over, in hopes of holding us fast till morning, while the other boats were to tie up to trees along the river bank.

As soon as the anchor fastened itself in the river bottom, the boat gave a little lurch or side motion, when the cable tore away all the frame-work around the deck, causing a great alarm. Several little black children were on deck at the time, and as it had now become quite dark, it could not be ascertained, in the excitement of the moment, whether any of them had been thrown into the water. Fortunately none were missing. During our confusion, Captain Osmun's boat passed ours, a few minutes after the accident, and we soon passed him, he hailing us, saying that he was entangled in the top of a large tree, which had caved into the river, and requested the small row-boat to assist him. Uncle Forman immediately dispatched the two mechanics, with the small boat, to his assistance. Osmun got clear of the tree without injury, and the two mechanics rowed hard, almost all night, before they overtook him. Mrs. Forman and daughters braved out our trying situation very firmly.

After we lost our anchor, Uncle Forman took a chair, and seated himself on the forecastle, like a pilot, and I took the helm. He kept watch, notifying me when to change the direction of the boat. When he cried out to me, " port your helm," it was to keep straight in the middle of the stream; if to bear to the left, he would cry out, " starboard; " if to the right, " larboard." I was not able to manage the helm alone, and had a man with me to assist in pulling as directed. Uncle Forman and I were the only ones of our party who understood sailor's terms. Ours was a perilous situation till we landed at Wheeling; it was the most distressing night I ever experienced.

The next morning, all our boats landed at Wheeling, Virginia, rated at ninety-six miles from Pittsburg. Here we obtained a large steering oar for the keel-boat, as the strong current kept the rudder from acting, without the application of great strength. Having adjusted matters, we set out again. We seldom ventured to land on our journey, for fear of lurking Indians.

One day, we discovered large flocks of wild turkeys flying about in the woods on shore. The blacksmith, who was a fine, active young man, asked Uncle Forman to set him on shore, and give him a chance to kill some of them. The little boat was manned, and taking his rifle and a favorite dog, he soon landed. But he had not been long on shore, before he ran back to the river's bank, and made signs for the boat to come and take him on board. When safely among his friends, he said that he came to a large fire, and, from appearances, he supposed a party of Indians was not far off. He, however, lost his fine dog, for he dared not call him.

We landed and stopped at Marietta, at the mouth of the Muskingum, where was a United States garrison. Some of the officers were acquainted with the family. It was a very agreeable occurrence to meet with old acquaintances in such a dreary place. The young ladies were good singers, and entertained the officers awhile with their vocal music. This night, we felt secure in sleeping away the fatigues of the journey. Governor St. Clair had his family here. There were a few other families, also; but all protected by the troops. I believe there was no other settlement * until we arrived at Fort Washington, now Cincinnati, some three hundred miles below Marietta.

A few hundred yards above Fort Washington, we landed our boats, when Uncle Forman, Colonel Wyckoff, and I went on shore, and walked up to head-quarters, to pay our respects to General Harmar, the commander of our troops in the North-western Territory. The general received us with much politeness. As we were about taking leave of him, he kindly invited us to remain and take a family dinner with him, observing to Uncle, that we should have the opportunity of testing the deliciousness of what he may never have partaken before—the haunch of

---

* Mr. Forman forgot to mention Limestone, now Maysville, Kentucky, some sixty miles above Cincinnati, an older settlement by some four years than Marietta or Cincinnati. Perhaps it was passed in the night, and unobserved. And Columbia, too, at the mouth of the Little Miami, about six miles above Cincinnati, and a few months its senior in settlement.

a fine buffalo. It being near dining hour, the invitation was, of course, accepted. As the general and lady were acquainted with Uncle and Aunt Forman in Philadelphia, they very politely extended their kindness by asking that Uncle, Aunt, and their family, together with Colonel Wyckoff and Brother-in-law Scudder and Captain Osmun, would spend the next day with them, which was accepted with great pleasure. General Harmar directed where to move our little fleet, so that all should be safe under military guard. We then returned to our boats, and conveyed them down to the appointed place.

The next morning, after breakfast, and after attending to our toilets, we repaired to General Harmar's headquarters, where we were all received most cordially. Our company consisted of Mr. and Mrs. Forman, their three daughters, and Master David Forman, Miss Church, Captain Osmun, S. S. Forman, Colonel Wyckoff, and Mr. Scudder—eleven in all.

Mrs. Forman and Mrs. Harmar resembled each other as much as though they were sisters. The general invited some of his officers to share his hospitalities, also, and we had a most sumptuous dinner and tea. Before it was quite dark, we took leave of our hospitable friends. I had the honor of a seat at the table next to the general. While at dinner, the officer of the day called on General Harmar for the countersign, so as to place out the sentinels. Captain Kirby,* of the army, who dined

---

* Neither the *Dictionary of the Army*, the *MS. Harmar Papers*, nor the *Journal of Major Denny*, who was then an aide to General Harmar, make any mention of a Captain Kirby. It is probable, that William Kersey was the officer referred to. He served in New Jersey during the Revolution, rising from a private to a

with us, was directed by the general to accompany us on our return to our boats. Just before we came to the sentinel, Captain Kirby asked us to halt, until he could advance and give the countersign, which is done with much prudence. I sauntered along, and happened to hear the challenge by the guard, and the reply of the captain. The countersign was, I believe, "Forman."

In the morning, Captain Osmun said to me, that, after paying our respects to General Harmar, he wanted me to accompany him to the quarters of the other officers, as he probably knew all of them; that they were old continental officers retained in service, and he added: "They all know your brother, Colonel Jonathan Forman,* of the Revolution, and will be glad to see you

---

captaincy by brevet at the close of the war. At this period, early in 1790, he was a lieutenant. Probably, by courtesy of his rank and title in the Revolution, he was called captain. He attained that rank the following year; major, in 1794; and died, March 21, 1809.

* Jonathan Forman was born October 16, 1755; was educated at Princeton College, where he was a fellow-student with James Madison, and entering the army in 1776 served as captain for five years, during which he participated in Sullivan's campaign against the hostile Six Nations; and, promoted to the rank of major in 1781, he served under La Fayette in Virginia; and early in 1783 he was made a lieutenant colonel, and continued in the army till the end of the war. He headed a regiment against the whisky insurgents of West Pennsylvania in 1794, and two years later he removed to Cazenovia, N. Y., where he filled the position of supervisor, member of the legislature and brigadier-general in the militia. He married Miss Mary Ledyard, of New London, Conn., who "went over her shoe tops in blood," in the barn where the wounded lay, the morning after Arnold's descent on New London and Fort Griswold, on Groton Heights, where

on his account." We, accordingly, after our interview with General Harmar, went to their quarters. They recollected Captain Osmun, and he introduced me, when they welcomed me most cordially, and made many inquiries after my brother.

I think it was in the autumn of 1790 that General Harmar was defeated by the Indians, and most of these brave officers were killed. At that period officers wore three-cornered hats, and by that means nearly all of them were singled out and killed, as they could be so easily distinguished from others.

Some distance above Fort Washington, the Scioto river empties into the Ohio. Near this river was a cave, which the whites had not discovered till after Harmar's defeat. Here the Indians would sally out against boats ascending the Ohio. A canoe passed us the day before we passed the Scioto, which had been fired into at that point, one man having been shot through the shoulder, another through the calf of the leg, while the third escaped unhurt. When these poor fellows arrived at Fort Washington, they waited for us. After our arrival, understanding that we were going to tarry a day, they set off. Harmar's defeat caused a French settlement near the Scioto to be broken up;* some of them were killed by the Indians.

---

her uncle, Colonel William Ledyard, was killed in cold blood after his surrender. General Forman died at Cazenovia, May 25, 1809, in his sixty-fourth year, and his remains repose in the beautiful cemetery at that place.

*The Gallipolis settlement was much annoyed by the Indians; some of the poor French settlers were killed, others

I must mention an anecdote about my friend, Captain Osmun. At the battle of Long Island, and capture of New York by the British, many American prisoners were taken, Captain Osmun among them. He pretended to be a little acquainted with the profession of physic, but he never studied it, and could bleed, draw teeth, etc. A German officer had a very sick child, the case baffling the skill of all the English and German physicians, and the child's recovery was given up as hopeless. At last it was suggested to call in the rebel doctor. So Osmun was sent for. He suppressed as well as he could his half-comical, half-quizzical expression, and assumed a serious look; felt of the child's pulse, and merely said he would prepare some pills and call again. He accordingly did so, giving the necessary directions, and promised to call at the proper time to learn the effect. When he called the third time the child had grown much better, and finally recovered. He said that all he did for the little sufferer was to administer a little powder-post, mixed up with ryebread, made into little pills. He said he knew they could do no harm, if they did no good, and regarded himself as only an instrument in the hands of the Almighty in saving the child's life. The father of the child gave him almost a handful of guineas. Prior to this occurrence he had, while a prisoner, suffered for the necessaries of life, but thenceforward he was able to procure needful comforts till his exchange.

The next morning, after our entertainment by Gen-

---

abandoned the place, but the settlement was maintained, despite all their trials and sufferings.

eral Harmar and lady, we renewed our journey, floating rapidly down the Belle Riviere. Nothing of moment occurred till our arrival at Louisville, at the Falls of the Ohio. The weather now grew so severely cold, in the latter part of January, 1790, that the river became blocked with ice. Here we laid up, disembarked, and took a house in the village, the front part of which was furnished for a store, which exactly suited us, and which was gratuitously offered to Uncle Forman by a Mr. Rhea, of Tennessee. We were remarkably fortunate in this respect, both here and at Pittsburg.

Here I opened a store from our stock of goods, and took tobacco in payment, which was the object in bringing the merchandise. Louisville then contained about sixty dwelling-houses. Directly opposite was Fort Jefferson,* which was, I believe, only a captain's command. At the Great Miami was Judge Symmes's settlement,†

---

* This is evidently an error of memory; it was known as Fort Steuben, located where Jeffersonville now is.

† Trivial circumstances sometimes change the fate of nations, and so it would seem they do of cities also. North Bend might have become the great commercial metropolis of the Miami country, instead of Cincinnati, but for an affair of the heart, if we may credit the tradition preserved by Judge Burnet in his *Notes on the North-western Territory*. Ensign Francis Luce had been detailed, with a small force, for the protection of the North Bend settlement, and to locate a suitable site for a block-house. While the ensign was keenly but very leisurely on the lookout for a proper location, he made a discovery far more interesting to him—a beautiful black-eyed lady, the wife of one of the settlers. Luce became infatuated with her charms, and her hus-

which dragged heavily along at that time, having been allowed only a sergeant's command for its protection.

Besides Symmes', there was no other settlement between Cincinnati and Louisville, except that of a French gentleman named Lacassangue, a few miles above Louisville, who began a vineyard on the Indian side of the river;

band, seeing the danger to which he was exposed if he remained where he was, resolved at once to remove to Cincinnati.

The gallant ensign was equal to the unexpected emergency, for he now began to discover what he had not discovered before, that North Bend was not, after all, so desirable a locality for the contemplated block-house as Cincinnati, and forthwith apprised Judge Symmes of these views, who strenuously opposed the movement. But the judge's arguments were not so effective as the sparkling eyes of the fair dulcinea then at Cincinnati. And so Luce and his military force were transplanted in double-quick time to Cincinnati; and where the troops were the settlers congregated for their protection and safety. And so, the Queen City of the West followed the fortunes of this unnamed forest queen, who so completely beguiled the impressible ensign.

In this case there was no ten years' war, as in the case of the beautiful Spartan dame, which ended in the destruction of Troy; but, by Luce's infatuation and removal, North Bend was as much fated as though the combined Indians of the North-west had blotted it out of existence. Soon after this portentious removal, Luce, on May 1, 1790, resigned from the army—whether on account of his fair charmer, history fails to tell us. This romantic story has been doubted by some, but Judge Burnet was an early settler of Cincinnati, and had good opportunities to get at the facts; and when I met the judge, fully forty years ago, he seemed not the man likely to indulge in romancing. That General Harmar, in forwarding Luce's resignation to the War Office, seemed particularly anxious that it should be accepted, would seem to imply that, for this intrigue, or some other cause, the general was desirous of ridding the service of him.

and one day Indians visited it, killing his people, and destroying his vines.* Mr. Lacassangue was a polite, hospitable man, and gave elegant dinners.

A nephew of Mrs. Washington of the name of Dand-

---

* Michael Lacassangue, a Frenchman of education, settled in Louisville as a merchant prior to March, 1789, when General Harmar addressed him as a merchant there. He located a station on the northern shore of the Ohio, three miles above Fort Steuben, now Jeffersonville, where he had purchased land in the Clark grant. In a MS. letter of Captain Joseph Ashton, commanding at Fort Steuben, addressed to General Harmar, April 3, 1790, these facts are given relative to the attack on Lacassangue's station. That on the preceding March 29th, the Indians made their attack, killing one man. There were only two men, their wives, and fourteen children in the station. Word was immediately conveyed to Captain Ashton of their situation, who detached a sergeant and fourteen men to their relief, and who arrived there, Captain Ashton states, in sixteen minutes after receiving intelligence of the attack. The Indians, three in number, had decamped, and were pursued several miles until their trail was lost on a dry ridge. The families were removed to Fort Steuben, and thus the station was, for a time, broken up.

Mr. Lacassangue must have been quite a prominent trader at Louisville in his day. About the first of June, 1790, Colonel Vigo, an enterprising trader of the Illinois country, consigned to him 4,000 pounds of lead, brought by Major Doughty from Kaskaskia. Mr. Lacassangue made efforts, in after years, to give character to his new town of Cassania—a name evidently coined out of his own—hoping from its more healthful situation, and better location for the landing of vessels destined to pass the Falls, to supplant Louisville. The little place, General Collot says, had in 1796, when he saw it, "only two or three houses, and a store." The ambitious effort was a vain one, and Cassania soon became lost to the geographical nomenclature of the country. Mr. Lacassangue died in 1797.

ridge lived with Mr. Lacassangue. When I returned to Philadelphia, I there met him again; he resided at General Washington's. While the Dandridge family stayed at Louisville, they received much attention. It was the custom of the citizens, when any persons of note arrived there, to get up a ball in their honor. They would choose managers; circulate a subscription paper to meet the expenses of the dance. Every signer, except strangers, must provide his partner, see her safe there and home again.

We had scarcely got located before a subscription paper was presented to Uncle Forman and myself. But the first ball after our arrival proved a failure, owing to the inclemency of the weather, so that no ladies could attend. General Wilkinson happened in town, and though he and Uncle Forman stayed but a little while, the young blades were disposed for a frolic. Some time before this a ball was tendered to General St. Clair, when the youngsters had a row, and destroyed the most of the breakable articles that the house afforded. But such instances of rudeness occurred only when no ladies were present.

Not long after the failure on account of the weather, the scheme for a dance was renewed, and, at length, we had an elegant collection of southern fair. The ball was opened by a minuet by Uncle Forman and a southern lady—Aunt Forman did not dance. This was the last time, I believe, that I saw that elegant dance performed. Then two managers went around with numbers on paper in a hat—one going to the ladies, the other to the gentlemen. When the manager calls for lady No. 1, the lady drawing that number stands up, and is led upon the floor, awaiting for gentleman No. 1, who, when called, takes his place, and is introduced by the manager to the lady. So they proceed with the drawing of couples until the floor is full for the dance.

I, in my turn, was drawn, and introduced to my dancing partner from Maryland, and we were called to the first dance. This lady happened to be acquainted with Uncle Forman's oldest son, General Thomas Marsh Forman, which circumstance rendered our casual meeting all the more agreeable. The officers of the garrison over the river generally attended, and they brought the military music along. I became well acquainted with the officers. Dr. Carmichael,* of the army, used often to come over and sit in my store.

It was the last of February, I believe, when Uncle Forman and his little fleet took their departure from Louisville, destined for the Natchez country. The river was now free from ice. There subsequently came a report, that when they reached what was called the low country, below the Cumberland and Tennessee rivers, they were captured by the Indians. I was in a painful suspense for a long time, and until I heard from them.

While Uncle Forman and party were sojourning in Louisville, there was, it appears, a white man there, who learned the names of Ezekiel Forman and Captain Osmun, their place of destination, and all about them. This fellow was a decoyer, who lived among the Indians, and whose business it was to lure boats ashore for pur-

---

* Dr. John F. Carmichael, from New Jersey, entered the army in September, 1789, and, with the exception of a few months, retained his position till his resignation in June, 1804.

poses of murder and robbery. At some point below the mouth of the Tennessee, this renegade saw the boats approaching, ran on the beech, imploring, upon his bended knees, that Mr. Forman, calling him by name, would come ashore and take him on board, as he had just escaped from the Indians. Mr. Forman began to steer for his relief, when Captain Osmun, who was a little way in the rear, hailed Uncle, warning him to keep in the middle of the stream, as he saw Indians in hiding behind trees along the bank where the wily decoyer was playing his treacherous part. Giving heed to this admonition, Uncle Forman kept clear of the dangerous shore.

Then an old Indian, finding that his plot was exposed, ran down to the beach, hailing the boats: "Where you go?" It is not clear what could have been the Indian's motive in making a display of himself, and seeking the information already known to his renegade associate. But for the circumstance of Captain Osmun being in the rear, and discovering the exposed Indians screened behind trees, the whole party might have been lured on shore and massacred. It seems that, after boats entered the Mississippi, they were not molested by the Indians, as they were not at war with the Spaniards.

I was left in Louisville, with a store of goods. When I had disposed of them, I was directed to join Uncle Forman at Natchez; but some considerable time was necessary to trade off my stock, and convert it into tobacco. I spent my time very pleasantly at Louisville. The southern people are remarkably friendly to strangers. One family, in particular, Mr. and Mrs. Ashby, were as kind to me as though I had been their own son. They soon called on Uncle and Aunt Forman, showing all possible attention, and soon became quite familiar.

One day, Mr. Ashby called, and inquired of Aunt for "*old* Mr. Forman." "I tell you, Mr. Ashby," Mrs. Forman laughingly replied, "you shall not call my husband *old*. Please to refer to him as Mr. Forman, and our nephew as Mr. Sam. Forman." Mr. Ashby took the suggestion in good part, and promised ready obedience. After Uncle and Aunt Forman left for the Natchez country, Mrs. Ashby would come to my store like a mother, and inquire into the condition of my lodgings, and sent bed and bedding, and had a kind old woman examine my trunk, taking out all my clothing, first airing and then nicely replacing them, and kindly did all my washing during my stay. Mr. Ashby had a farm a little way out of town, but he and his family came in very often. Mrs. Ashby never came without making me a motherly call, and looking over my clothing to see if any repairs were needed. I never parted with briefly-made acquaintances with so much regret.

I became very intimate with a Mr. Smith, from New York, a young gentleman about my own age. The Virginians, as were most of the Louisville people, were very fond of dancing. Smith and I agreed to let each other know when a hop was in agitation, and they were very frequent. When notified by him of one such occasion, I apologized for not being able to go, as I had no suitable pumps. "You have purchased," said he, "a parcel of elegant moccasins for your New York ladies. You don a pair, and I will another." "Good! good!" we mutually ejaculated. So we engaged our favorite partners, and attended the ball. It was something new to appear in such an assembly decked off in such Indian gear; but they were much admired, and, at the next dance, almost all appeared in moccasins. So, it seems, we led the ton, and introduced a new fashion.

There was but one tavern and one boarding-house in the place. The boarding-house was kept by a Dr. Walter, who was also the pilot to take boats over the Falls; and he was, moreover, a great hunter and fisherman. One day in April, I think, at some public festival, several of our boarders, the leader was the Commissary of the Army, proposed to have what they called *a setting*, and asked me to join them. I had often heard the commissary relate his exploits—drinking egg-nog was then all the go. I declined to share in the frolic, fearing the influence of these southern blades on such occasions. In he course of the night, I was alarmed by the rattling of stones thrown against my store-door and window-shutters. At first, I thought it might be Indians. The clatter was kept up, and the glass windows all broken. I finally concluded that it was the work of the egg-nog party. Not only were my windows completely shattered, but my store door was broken open by the pelting of large stones.

These egg-nog disturbers served Captain Thomas, the landlord, in the same way as they had done me. The next morning, when we all met at the breakfast table at our boarding-house, scarcely a word was spoken during the meal. As I went out of the door, passing my friend, the commissary, I asked him if he would direct my windows glazed, and some little carpenter work done. He pretended to be astonished how they should have been broken. I made no reply, but walked back to my store, only looked at him and smiled. In the afternoon, at Captain Thomas's, the business assumed almost a tragical form—dirks were nearly drawn; however, it was amicably settled.

The next morning these gentlemen asked me if I would be satisfied if my windows and door were made whole. I answered in the affirmative, and asked them whether they had not acted very imprudently, situated as we were on the frontiers in time of Indian warfare. "You know," said I, "that it was but a little time since that Captain Thomas and some others saw Indians in the night making, as they supposed, for my store, when I kept it up by Bear Grass creek; and a few people got together in the night, and followed the Indian trail ou' of the village without alarming me. The Indians evidently thought themselves discovered, and retired, hence I escaped. In consequence of this alarm, I immediately moved from that place to the center of the village, into the corner building opposite the tavern."

It was observed one Sunday morning, soon after starting my store, that it was not opened on that day, as other establishments were; and I was asked why I kept my store closed—that Sunday had not crossed the mountains, and that I was the first person who kept his store shut on that day. I told them that I brought the Sabbath with me. It so happened that I had the honor of being the first to observe the day in Louisville.

Directly opposite to me a billiard table was kept. It was customary at the south for ladies to indulge in billiards, considering it a genteel and healthful amusement. During the morning hours, a few ladies used to honor me with a call, when I would spend a little while in that pleasant recreation; but I never gambled, and ladies' company is always more agreeable than gentlemen's. Besides, if you play with gentlemen, it is apt to lead to gambling; and it was consequently better to pay for the use of the table with ladies, when one improves in manners from their refinement.

One day Captain Thomas brought a little negro boy to my store, tendering me his services while I remained in Louisville; that he should be of no expense to me, but live at home, and come over regularly and do my chores, tote water, sweep my store, clean my shoes, etc. The captain explained that he had another boy of about the same age and size, and that one was better than both. I had a spruce colored barber, who was also a tailor, the pleasure of whose company I occasionally had in helping out in my labors.

Sometime about the latter part of May, perhaps, four tobacco boats arrived at Louisville on their way to New Orleans, under the respective command of Captain Andrew Bayard, Captain Winters, and Captain Gano, of New York, and Captain January, of Kentucky. Captain Bayard's boat received some injury in passing over the Falls of the Ohio, and he had to unload to repair damages. I had been some time negotiating with a rich planter, Mr. Buckner, of Louisville. After I had heard of the accident to Captain Bayard's boat, Mr. Buckner came into the village. I got him in my store, locked the door, and told him that now was the time to close our long-talked-of trade, so that I could have the company of this descending fleet. After spending the night in conversation, I gave up my bed to Mr. Buckner, and threw down some blankets and coarse clothes for my own lodging.

To make a long story short, we effected a trade—closing out my store of goods to him. He bought me a tobacco boat, loaded her with this product of the country, and got matters and things arranged so that I was ready to accompany the descending fleet. Of these tobacco traders, I was partially acquainted with Mr. Bayard. I had at Louisville a competitor in trade, a young Irish gentleman, but he could not succeed.

My boat was loaded below the Falls, and by some means the hands suffered her to break from her fastenings, and went a mile or two down stream before they brought her to. I put my blanket on board of Mr. Bayard's boat, and got on board with him, and took my tea with him. In the evening, being moonlight, my canoe, with an old sailor, came for me. I took some blankets and wrapped them around my arms carelessly. I jumped into the canoe; and the sailor, it seems, had taken a little too much whisky, so that when he pushed off from Mr. Bayard's boat, in order to clear its bow, he leaned over so far as to make the canoe dip water; and, in recovering his position, he leaned so far the other way that the canoe filled. My arms being entangled with the blankets, I was totally helpless. Mr. Bayard's hands jumped into their small boat, came to my rescue, and saved me from a watery grave.

Partly from economy, and partly from lack of time to secure another hand, I attempted to manage my tobacco boat, which was somewhat smaller than the usual size, with less than the usual supply of boatmen. This made it come hard on me, whose unskilled strength was but half that of an ordinary man. I had this old sailor with me for one watch, and an old North-western man and a Jerseyman for another. The boats would follow the current, except when passing islands, when the men must all beat their oars. I believe the old sailor, while on board, was a little deranged. After I discharged him at Natchez, he was found, I was told, in the woods, dead.

Nothing of any moment occurred while descending the Ohio, until we reached Fort Massac, an old French fortification, about thirty miles above the mouth of the Ohio. It was a beautiful spot. All of the captains, and some of the hands, with a small boat, went on shore, while our tobacco boats glided gently along. When we landed, we separated in squads, and visited the old deserted ramparts, which appeared quite fresh. It was in the afternoon, just after a refreshing shower. Those first arriving at the intrenchment, espied a fresh moccasin track. We all looked at it, and then at each other, and, without uttering a word, all faced about, and ran as fast as possible for the little boat. Some hit its locality, while others struck the river too high up, and others, too low.

Those of us who missed our way concluded, in our fright, that the Indians had cut us off; and no one had thought to take his rifle but me, and I feared that I should be the first to fall. After we were all safe on one of the tobacco boats, we recovered our speech, and each one told how he felt, and what he thought, during our flight to the boats. This locality of Fort Massac, we understood, was the direct way from the Ohio, in that country, to St. Louis, and probably the track we saw was that of some lonely Indian; and, judging from its freshness, the one who made it was as much frightened from our numbers as we were at our unexpected discovery.

I will note a little circumstance that occurred during our passage down the Ohio. One day, I was ahead of the fleet, when one of the boats passed by suddenly, when we observed by the woods that we were standing still—evidently aground, or fast on something below the surface. I gave notice to the boats behind to come on, and take position between my boat and shore, hoping, by this means, to raise a temporary swell in the river, and, by fastening a rope to my boat, and extending along beside the others, and making the other end fast to a tree on shore, be enabled to get loose.

While thus engaged, we heard a whistle, like that of a quail. Some observed that quail never kept in the woods, and we felt some fear that it might be Indians; but we continued our efforts at the rope, and the boat was soon so far moved that we discovered that we were fast upon a planter—that is, the body of a tree firmly embedded in the river bottom. At last, the men could partly stand upon it, and, with a hand-saw, so weakened it that it broke off, and we were released.

Another dangerous obstruction is a tree becoming undermined and falling into the river, and the roots fastening themselves in the muddy bottom, while, by the constant action of the current, the limbs wear off, and the body keeps sawing up and down with great force, rising frequently several feet above the water, and then sinking as much below. These are called "sawyers," and often cause accidents to unsuspecting navigators.

When we arrived at the mouth of the Ohio, we stopped. I fastened my boat to trees, and the other boats did likewise. We kept watch, with an ax in hand, to cut the fastenings in case of a surprise by Indians. Here were marks of buffalo having rested. Where the waters of the Mississippi and Ohio mingle, they look like putting dirty soap-suds and pure water together. So we filled all our vessels that were water-tight, for fear we might suffer for want of good water on our voyage. But we found out, afterward, that the Mississippi was very good water, when filtered.

After we got all arranged, the second day after we embarked, the captains agreed that we would, in rotation, dine together, which rendered our journey more pleasant. Mr. Bayard's and my boat were frequently fastened together while descending the Ohio, but on the Mississippi, from the turbulence of the stream, it was not possible to do so. The first day that we entered the Mississippi, we discharged all our rifles and pistols, as we were then out of danger from the hostile Indians. In the afternoon, we had a strong wind ahead, which made a heavy sea, accompanied with thunder and lightning. The waves ran so high that we felt in danger of foundering. The forward boat pulled hard for shore, which we all followed.

Presently, we saw an Indian canoe pulling for that boat. I asked my North-western man what that meant. He looked wild, but did not know what to make of it. I directed the men to pull away, and I would keep an eye upon the suspicious visitors, and at the same time load our rifles and pistols again. Reaching the advanced boat, the Indians were kindly received, and no fighting; and, instead of hostile demonstrations, they lent a hand in rowing.

After much hard work, we at length all effected a landing

in safety. We then prepared for dinner. It so happened that it was my turn to receive the captains at dinner. Having a large piece of fresh beef—enough and to spare, I invited three of our copper-faces to dine with us. Dinner over, Captain Gano set the example of *pitching the fork* into the beef, as we used, in our school days, to pitch the fork into the ground. So the Indians, one after the other, imitated the captain, and very dextrously pitched their forks also into the beef, thinking, probably, that it was a white man's ceremony that should be observed.

After dinner, at the conclusion of the pitching incident, I mixed some whisky and water in the only glass I had, and handed it to one of the captains: and then repeating it, filling the tumbler equally alike in quantity, handed it in succession to the others. When I came to the Indians, not knowing their relative rank, I happened to present the glass to the lowest in order, as I discovered by his declining it: but when I came to the leader, he took the offering, and reaching out his hand to me in a genteel and graceful manner, shook mine heartily; and then repeated the cordial shake with each of the others, not omitting his own people, and then drank our healths as politely, I imagine, as Lord Chesterfield could have done. The other Indians were similarly treated, and, in turn, as gracefully acknowledged the compliment. They all appeared much pleased with their reception.

This ceremony over, our men asked leave to visit the opposite side of the river, where these Indians had a large encampment. This granted, they all went to get their rifles. The Indians seemed to understand etiquette and politeness, and objected to the men going armed. But, instead of speaking to the men, they addressed the captains of the boats, saying: "We have no objections to your men going among our people, if they don't take their rifles. We came among you as friends, bringing no arms along." We, of course, told our men to leave their rifles behind. They did so. Returning, they reported that there were a good many Indians there. By some means, some of our men must have let the Indians have *la tafia*—a cheap variety of rum distilled from molasses. At all events, they became very much intoxicated, "and we," said the visitors, " were very apprehensive of difficulty; but a squaw told us that the Indians could not fight, as she had secreted all their knives, and we were very much relieved when morning appeared, so we could bid good-by to our new acquaintances."

The next day we arrived at *L' Anse a la Graisse*, which place, or adjoining it, bears the name of New Madrid, which is the American part of the little village settled under the auspices of Colonel George Morgan. Uncle Forman wrote me by all means to call at this Spanish post, as he had left my name with the genteel commandant there, who would expect to see me. In the morning, after breakfast, we all prepared our toilets preparatory to paying our respects to the officer of the place. The captains did me the honor of making me the foreman of the party, as my name would be familiar to the commandant. I regret that I have forgotten his name.* We made our call at as early an hour

---

* In July, 1789, less than a year before, Lieutenant Pierre Foucher, with four officers and thirty soldiers, had been sent

as we could, so that we might pursue our voyage without any unnecessary waste of time.

Arrived at the gate, the guard was so anxious to trade his tame raccoon with our men that he scarcely took any notice of us. We went to head-quarters; there was but little ceremony. When we were shown into the commander's presence, I stepped toward him a little in advance of my friends, and announced my name. I was most cordially and familiarly received. Then I introduced my friends, mentioning their respective places of residence. After a little conversation, we rose to retire, when the commandant advanced near me, and politely asked me to dine with him an hour after twelve o'clock, and bring my accompanying friends with me. I turned to the gentlemen for their concurrence, which they gave, when we all returned to our boats.

I then observed to my friends that the commandant would expect some present from us—such was the custom—and what should it be? Mr. Bayard, I believe, asked me to suggest some thing in our power to tender. I then remarked, that, as we had a plenty of good hams, that we fill a barrel, and send them to our host; that they might prove as acceptable as any thing. The proposition met the approval of all, and the hams were accordingly sent at once, with perhaps an accompanying note.

---

from New Orleans to establish a post at this place, as stated in *Gayarre's Louisiana*, 1854, p. 268. It is generally asserted that this settlement was commenced as early as 1780; but the Spanish census of Louisiana, both in 1785 and 1788, make no mention of the place.

At one hour after twelve o'clock, I well remember, we found ourselves comfortably seated at the hospitable board of the Spanish commandant, who expressed much delight at receiving our fine present. He gave us an elegant dinner in the Spanish style, and plenty of good wine and liquors, and coffee without cream. The commandant, addressing me, while we were indulging in the liquids before us, said that we must drink to the health of the ladies in our sweet liquors. "So," said he, "we will drink the health of the Misses Forman"—my worthy cousins, who had preceded us in a visit to this garrison.

After dinner, the commandant invited us to take a walk in the fine prairies. He said he could drive a coach-and-four through these open woods to St. Louis. There came up a thunder-storm and sharp lightning, and he asked me what I called that in English, and I told him, when he pleasantly observed: "You learn me to talk English, and I will learn you French." Returning to head-quarters, we took tea, and then got up to take our final leave. "O, no!" said he, "I can't spare you, gentlemen. I'm all alone. Please to come to-morrow, one hour after twelve, and dine again with me." So, at the appointed time, we were on hand again. The same kind hospitality was accorded us as on the preceding day.

In the evening, we thought we should surely tender the last farewell. But no; we must come again, for the third day, to enjoy his good company and delightful viands. That evening, there was a Spanish dance, all common people making up the company—French, Canadians, Spaniards, Americans. The belle of the room was Cherokee Katy, a beautiful little squaw, dressed in Spanish style, with a turban on her head, and decked off very handsomely. On these occasions, a king and queen were chosen to be sovereigns for the next meeting. The commandant was asked to honor them by taking a partner, and sharing in the mazy dance, which, of course, he declined; and we also had an invitation, but declined also. The commandant said he always went to these happy gatherings, and sat a little while, and once, he added, he played a little while on his own violin, for his own and their amusement.

He expressed much regret at parting with us. He said he was so lonesome. He was a man not over thirty, I suppose, highly accomplished, and spoke pretty good English. I fear he was, in after years, swallowed up in the earthquake,* which destroyed many; among them, I

---

* We learn, from Gayarre's *History of the Spanish Domination of Louisiana*, that, in July, 1789, Pierre Foucher, a lieutenant of the regiment of Louisiana, was sent, with two sergeants, two corporals, and thirty soldiers, to build a fort at New Madrid, and take the civil and military command of that district, with instructions to govern those new colonists in such a way as to make them feel that they had found among the Spaniards the state of ease and comfort of which they were in quest.

Colonel John Pope, in his *Tour Through the Western and Southern States*, states, under date, March 12, 1791: "Breakfasted and dined with Signor Pedro Foucher, commandant at New Madrid. The garrison consists of about ninety men, who are well supplied with food and raiment. They have an excellent train of artillery, which appears to be their chief defense. Two regular companies of musqueteers, with charged bayonets, might take this place. Of this opinion is the commandant himself, who complains that he is not sufficiently supported. He is a Creole of

believe, a Mr. Morris, who was a brother to Mrs. Hurd; a Mr. Lintot, from Natchez, who was a passenger with me from New Orleans to Philadelphia.

On our entering the Mississippi, we had agreed that the foremost boat should fire a gun as a token for landing, if they saw a favorable spot after the middle of the afternoon. It was not possible to run in safety during the night. It so happened that every afternoon we had a thunder shower and head wind.

Nothing special occurred, I believe, till our arrival at Natchez. There was no settlement from *L'Anse à la Graisse* to *Bayou Pierre*, something like sixty miles above Natchez. At Bayou Pierre lived Colonel Bruin,*

French extraction, of Patagonian size, polite in his manners, and of a most noble presence."

Lieutenant Foucher must have left the country long before the great earthquake of 1811-12. The Spaniards evacuated their posts on the Mississippi to the north of 31st degree in 1798; and, two years later, transferred the country to France, and, in 1803, it was purchased by the United States.

*Colonel Peter Bryan Bruin, son of an Irish gentleman, who had become implicated in the Irish Rebellion of 1756, and confiscation and exile were his penalty. He brought with him to America his only son, who was reared a merchant. In the War of the Revolution, he entered Morgan's famous riflemen as a lieutenant, shared in the assault on Quebec, where he was made a prisoner, and confined in a prison ship, infected with small-pox, for six months. He was finally exchanged, and at length promoted to the rank of major, serving to the end of the war. Soon after settling near the mouth of Bayou Pierre, he was appointed alcalde, or magistrate, under the Spanish Government; and when the Mississippi Territory was organized, in 1798, he was appointed one of the three territorial judges, remaining in office until he resigned, in 1810. He lived till a good old age, was a devoted patriot, and a man of high moral character.

of the Virginia Continental line, who, after the war, took letters from General Washington to the governor of that country while it belonged to Spain, and secured a fine land grant. I once visited Colonel Bruin, with a gentleman from Natchez. That section of country is remarkably handsome, and the soil rich. The colonel's dwelling-house was on the top of a large mound, and his barn on another, near by. These mounds are common in the Ohio and Mississippi countries, and no tradition gives their origin.

While in Louisville, I bought a young cub bear, and kept him chained in the back room of my store. He was about a month or two old when I got him; and when I went down the river, I took him along to Natchez. When twelve or fifteen months old, he became very saucy; I only could keep him in subjection. When he became too troublesome, Uncle Forman had him killed, and invited several gentlemen to join him in partaking of his bear dinner.

When our little fleet of five boats first came in sight of the village of Natchez, it presented quite a formidable appearance, and caused a little alarm at the fort; the drum beat to arms, but the affright soon subsided. About this time, a report circulated that general somebody, I have forgotten his name, was in Kentucky raising troops destined against that country; but it all evaporated.*

---

* This refers to the proposed settlement at the Walnut Hills, at the mouth of the Yazoo, under the auspices of the famous Yazoo Company, composed mostly of prominent South Carolina and Georgia gentlemen. Dr. John O'Fallon, who subsequently married a sister of General George Rogers Clark, located at

Natchez was then a small place, with houses generally of a mean structure, built mostly on the low bank of the river, and on the hillside. The fort was on a handsome, commanding spot, on the elevated ground, from which was a most extensive view up the river, and over the surrounding country. The governor's house was not far from the garrison. Uncle Forman had at first hired a large house, about half-way up the hill from the landing, where he lived until he bought a plantation of five hundred acres on the bank of St. Catherine's creek, about four miles from Natchez. This he regarded as only a temporary abode, until he could become better acquainted with the country. The place had a small clearing and a log house on it, and he put up another log house to correspond with it, about fourteen feet apart, connecting them with boards, with a piazza in front of the whole. The usual term applied to such a structure was that it was "two pens and a passage." This connecting passage made a fine hall, and altogether gave it a good and comfortable appearance.

Boards were scarce, and I do not remember of seeing any saw or grist-mills in the country. Uncle Forman had a horse-mill, something like a cider-mill, to grind.

Louisville, Ky., as the agent and active partner in that region, and endeavored to enlist General Clark as the military leader of the enterprise; but it would appear that the general declined the command, and Colonel John Holder, a noted Kentucky pioneer and Indian fighter, was chosen in his place. But nothing was accomplished. The original grant was obtained by bribery, fraud, and corruption, from the Georgia Legislature; and a subsequent legislature repudiated the transaction, and ordered all the documents and records connected with it to be burned in the public square.

corn for family use. In range with his dwelling he built a number of negro houses, some distance off, on the bank of St. Catherine's creek. It made quite a pretty street. The little creek was extremely convenient. The negroes the first year cleared a large field for tobacco, for the cultivation of that article was the object of Mr. Forman's migration to that country.

After my arrival, and while sojourning at Natchez, Uncle Forman asked me if I intended to apply to the government for lands. I replied that I did not want any. He said he was glad of it, unless I remained in the country. He hinted something to the effect that one of the Spanish officers, who talked of leaving the country, had an elegant plantation, with negroes for its cultivation, and he thought of buying it, if I would stay and take it; that if I took land of government, and sold out, it might give umbrage to the governor, and I, being a relation, he suffer by it. I told him my father was loath to let me come away, and I promised that I would return if my life was spared me.

After this, Surveyor-General Dunbar,* much to my

---

* Sir William Dunbar, son of Sir Archibald Dunbar, was born at Elgin, Scotland, and received a superior education in Glasgow and London. On account of failing health, he obtained a stock of goods for the Indian trade; and, landing in Philadelphia in April, 1771, took his goods to Fort Pitt, and about 1773 he went to West Florida to form a plantation. He suffered much during the period of the Revolution, and in 1772 settled near Natchez, became chief surveyor under the Spanish Government, and in 1798 he was appointed astronomical commissioner on the part of Spain in establishing the boundary. He was shortly after appointed by Governor Sargeant, on the organization of Mississippi Territory, under the United States Government, chief judge of

surprise, called on me, and said that he brought the survey and map of my land, and presented a bill of sixty dollars for his services. I told him that I had not asked for land, nor had Governor Gayoso ever said any thing to me about land, nor did I want any. General Dunbar replied that the governor directed him to survey for Don Samuel S. Forman eight hundred acres of land, and that it was the best and most valuable tract that he knew of in the district, including a beautiful stream of water, with a gravelly bottom—rare in that country; that it was well located, near a Mr. Ellis, at the White Cliffs, and advised me by all means to take it. Uncle Forman happened to be absent, and I was in doubt what to do. At last I paid the bill and took the papers. The largest quantity that the Spanish Government gave to a young man who settled in that country was two hundred and forty acres, so the governor showed much friendship by complimenting me with so large a grant.

I must go back a little, and state that my good traveling companions, Messrs. Bayard, Gano, Winters, and January, parted from me, and continued their journey down the river. Uncle Forman had been acquainted with Mr. Bayard, in Philadelphia, and their meeting in a distant and foreign country was very gratifying. The interview was very brief, for Mr. Bayard and associates were anxious to pursue their voyage.

At Natchez we made many agreeable acquaintances.

---

the Court of Quarter Sessions. He corresponded with the most distinguished scientific men of his time, and contributed to the Transactions of the American Philosophical Society. He died in 1810, leaving many descendants.

Governor Gayoso, a bachelor, was very affable and pleasant, and had an English education. The fort-major, Stephen Minor,* was a Jerseyman from Princeton, and Mr. Hutchins,† a wealthy planter, was a brother to Thomas Hutchins, the geographer-general of the United States. His wife was a Conover, from near Freehold village, and knew more about Freehold than I did. Also a Mr. Moore, a wealthy planter, Mr. Bernard Lintot, who moved from Vermont before the war, and Mr. Ellis, a wealthy planter—all having large families, sons and daughters, very genteel and accomplished. These all lived from eight to fourteen miles from us.

In the village of Natchez resided Monsieur and Madam Mansanteo—Spanish Jews, I think—who were the most kind and hospitable of people. These families, in town and country, formed our principal associates. Governor Gayoso told us, after we moved out to St. Catherine, that there would always be a plate for us at his table.

The year 1790 was a very sickly one for unacclimated persons in the Natchez country. All our family adults

---

* Stephen Minor was a native of Pennsylvania, well-educated, and early made his way West; first to St. Louis, and then to New Orleans, and was soon appointed to official station by the Spanish Government, rising eventually to the governorship at Natchez, and so continuing till the evacuation of the country. He then became a citizen of the United States, and was useful to the country. He died in after years at Concord, Mississippi.

† Colonel Anthony Hutchins was a native of New Jersey; early migrated to North Carolina, and in 1772 explored the Natchez country, settling permanently at the White Apple village, twelve miles from Natchez, the following year, and survived the troubles of the Revolution, and died when past eighty years of age.

had more or less fever, and fever and ague. Uncle Forman was severely afflicted with gout—a lump almost as big as a small hen's egg swelled out at one of his elbows, with something of the appearance of chalk. Poor Betsey Church was taken with a fever, and died in a few days; a great loss to the family, having been a valuable and much respected member of it for many years. I was the only adult of the family who was not confined to the house with sickness.

Stephen Minor, the fort-major, married the eldest daughter of the planter, Mr. Ellis. Our family was much visited by the Spanish officers, who were very genteel men; and Major Minor was very intimate, and seemed to take much interest in us.

When the time was fixed for my departure, by the way of New Orleans, and thence by sea to Philadelphia, Uncle Forman said: "Well, you must direct Moses, the coachman, to get up the carriage, take two of your cousins with you, and take leave of all your good friends." The carriage, which had its top broken off crossing the mountains in Pennsylvania, had been fitted up in Natchez, with neat bannister work around the top of the body, which rendered it more convenient for the country. We sometimes took the family in it, and went out strawberrying over the prairies.

Cousins Augusta and Margaret accompanied me on my farewell tour. Ours was the first four-wheeled carriage that ever passed over those grounds—I can't say roads, for the highway was only what was called a bridle-path—all traveling at that day was on horseback. When we visited one place, some of our friends from another locality meeting us there would ascertain the day we designed visiting their house, that they might have the cane-brakes along the trail cleared away sufficient to permit the comfortable passage of the carriage; and we must, moreover, be on time, or some small gust of wind might again obstruct the passage. Our visits were all very pleasant save the unhappy part of the final bidding each other farewell.

During this excursion, Governor Gayoso had given permission for a Baptist clergyman to preach one Sunday, which was the first time a protestant minister had been allowed to hold religious services. The meeting was held at Colonel Hutchins'. We went from the residence of some friends in that vicinity. After service we were invited to stay and dine at Colonel Hutchins'. When we were ready to depart, all came out of the house to see us off, and I asked the ladies in a jocose way to join us in the ride, when they began to climb over the wheels as though they might endanger the safety of the carriage; but this frolicsome banter over, we took our departure. We spent several days in performing this friendly round of visits—by-gone days of happiness never to return.

When I was about leaving the country, Governor Gayoso asked me what I intended to do with my land. I replied, that if I did not return in a year or two, that his excellency could do what he pleased with it. Some years after, when I lived in Cazenovia, I contemplated going back, and went to my large chest, which had traveled with me from Pittsburgh to New Orleans, and thence in all my tramps and changes, where I supposed all my Spanish papers were safe in a little drawer; but, to my surprise, they were missing, and I never could tell what became of them, as I kept the chest locked, and retained the key. So vanished my eight hundred acres of valuable land in the promising Mississippi country.

On the arrival of Colonel Wyckoff, with his brother-in-law, Scudder, from Tennessee, preparations were made for our departure. Uncle Forman went down to New Orleans with us. It was in June, 1791, I believe, that we left Natchez. The parting with my kindred was most trying and affecting, having traveled and hazarded our lives together for so many hundred miles, and never expecting to meet again in this life. Many of the poor colored people, too, came and took leave of me, with tears streaming down their cheeks. Take them altogether, they were the finest lot of servants I ever saw. They were sensible that they were all well cared for—well fed, well clothed, well housed, each family living separately, and they were treated with kindness. Captain Osmun,* their overseer, was a kind-hearted man, and used

---

* Benajah Osmun served, as Mr. Forman has previously stated, at the defeat of General Washington's troops on Long Island, in August, 1776, when he was made a prisoner; he was then, apparently, a soldier in the ranks. On January 1, 1777, he was appointed a second lieutenant and quartermaster in Colonel Shreve's Second New Jersey regiment, which he subsequently resigned. In September, 1778, he again entered the army as an ensign in the second regiment; was a prisoner of war on April 25, 1780; made a lieutenant January 1, 1781, retiring at the close of the war with the brevet rank of captain.

In 1802, he was made lieutenant-colonel of the Adams county militia; and when Colonel Burr visited the country, in 1807, on his mysterious mission, he was the guest of Colonel Osmun, who was one of his two bondsmen for his appearance at court, for

them well. They had ocular proof of their happy situation when compared with their neighbor's servants. It was the custom of the country to exchange work ta times; and, one day, one of our men came to me, and said: "I don't think it is right to exchange work with these planters; for I can, with ease, do more work than any two of their men:" and added, "their men pound their corn over night for their next day's supply, and they are too weak to work." Poor fellows, corn was all they had to eat.

Uncle Forman and I stopped the first night with Mr. Ellis, at the White Cliffs, and next day embarked on board of a boat for New Orleans. On our way down we sometimes went on shore and took a bowl of chocolate for breakfast with some rich planter, a very common custom of the country. The night before our arrival at New Orleans we put up with a Catholic priest; some gentlemen of our company were well acquainted between Natchez and New Orleans, and had learned the desirable stopping places. The good priest received us kindly, gave us an excellent supper, plenty of wine, and was himself very lively. We took breakfast with him the next morning; and before our departure the priest came up to me with a silver plate in his hand, on which were two fine looking pears, which he tendered me. He looked at first very serious; but, remembering his good humor the previous evening, I suspected his fun had not yet all run out. I eyed him pretty close, and while thanking him, I rather

---

they were fellow officers in the Revolution. Colonel Osmun settled a plantation at the foot of Half Way hill, near Natchez, became wealthy, and there died, a bachelor, at a good old age.

hesitated, when he urged me to take them. I knew no pears grew in that country. I finally took one, weighed it in my hand, and looked at him, till he bursted out into a loud laugh. They were ingeniously wrought out of stone or marble, and looked exactly like pears. I brought them home and gave them to a friend.

Arriving in New Orleans, we took lodgings, and our first business was to wait on his excellency Governor Miro. Mr. Forman settling within his government with so large a number of people, under an arrangement with the Spanish ambassador at New York, Don Diego de Gardoque, gave him a high standing. Uncle Forman was in person a fine-looking man, very neat, prepossessing, and of genteel deportment, so that he was always much noticed.

As there was then no vessel in port destined for the United States, I had to delay a couple of weeks for one. At length the brig Navarre, Captain McFadden, made its appearance, and soon loaded for Philadelphia. There were a number of Americans in waiting, who engaged their passage with me, on this vessel. Uncle Forman did not leave the city until after the Navarre had taken its departure. He suggested that I should take a formal leave of Governor Miro and his secretary, Don Andre. The secretary was a large, fine-looking man. I politely asked him if he had any commands for the cape—Cape Francois, a fine town in the northern part of St. Domingo, usually dignified with the designation of the *The Cape*— for which port, I believe, the vessel cleared. "I know not," said the secretary, "to what cape you are going— only take good care of yourself."

After all were on board, the brig dropped down two or

three miles, where the passengers went ashore, and laid in provisions enough, the captain said, to have carried us to London after our arrival in Philadelphia. I may mention something about distances as computed in those days. From Natchez to New Orleans was called three hundred miles by water, and only one hundred and fifty by land. From New Orleans to the Balize, at the mouth of the Mississippi, was reckoned one hundred and five miles. It was said that such was the immense volume of the Mississippi river that it kept its course and muddy appearance for a league out at sea.

There were no ladies among the passengers. We entered into an arrangement that each passenger should, in rotation, act as caterer for the party for each day. It fell to my lot to lead off in this friendly service. We got along very nicely, and with a good deal of mirthful pleasure, for a couple of weeks, enjoying our viands and wine as comfortably as if at a regular boarding house. The captain's wife, however, was something of a drawback to our enjoyment. She was a vinegary looking creature, and as cross and saucy as her looks betokened, was low-bred, ill-tempered, and succeeded in making herself particularly disagreeable. During the pleasant weather portion of our voyage, she managed, without cause, to raise a quarrel with every passenger; and what added to her naturally embittered feeling, was that we only laughed at her folly.

When we arrived in sight of Cuba, the wind arose, and blew almost a hurricane, causing a heavy sea. We were in such danger of being cast away on the Florida reefs that the captain summoned all hands on deck for counsel. But, providentially, we escaped. For near two weeks no cooking could be done, and each one was thankful to take whatever he could obtain in one hand, and hold fast to something with the other, such was the rolling and pitching of our frail vessel. Most of the passengers were sea-sick; I was among the few who escaped from that sickening nausea. One night the rain was so heavy, the lightning so vivid, and thunder so tremendous, that the vessel trembled at every clap; when I went to my friend Wickoff, as well as others who were asleep, informing them that it was a moment of no little danger and excitement.

Captain McFadden was a most profane man. But during the hours of our distress and danger he became very mild and humble, but it lasted no longer than the storm. The vinegary Mrs. McFadden, too, was very sensibly affected during this trying period; for, standing in the companion-way, leading to the cabin, she very humbly and demurely said that she would go below and make her peace. We all thought she could not be too quick about it. She was a veritable Katharine, but he was not a Petruchio.

Before we arrived at the capes of the Delaware, an American sailor, who had made his escape from a British man-of-war at the mouth of the Mississippi, sickened and died on board our craft. When we got into the Delaware, the sailors took his remains on shore and gave them a decent sepulture. At length we reached Philadelphia in safety.

GENERAL INDEX.

Prefatory note	3
Memoir of Major S. S. Forman	5
Forman's narrative	5
Tunis Forman captures two Tories	6
Major Lee's strategy	6
British foray at Middletown Point	6, 7
Major Burrows's loss and captivity	7
Denise Forman's services	7
General David Forman	7
Germantown battle	7
Capture of a British sloop	8
A British and Tory scout	9
Services of Major Burrows	9
Major Burrows's narrow escape	9, 10
Denise Forman and Philip Freneau	10
Sufferings in British prison ships	10, 11
Captain Freneau's after-life	11, 12
Monmouth battle	12
Fugitives return to New York	12
British evacuate New York	13–15
Lieutenant-Colonel J. N. Cumming	14
Anthony Glean noticed	14
Washington parting with his officers	15
Washington and Franklin in Federal Convention	15
Washington's second inauguration	16
Major Forman settles at Cazenovia, N. Y.	17
His subsequent career	17, 18
His narrative—departure for the Ohio	19
Detention at Lancaster	20
Meeting Charley Morgan	22
Scant of funds for traveling	22

General Index.

Arrival at Pittsburg	23
Flat-l ottomed boats for the journey	23
Colonel Turnbull's entertainment	24
Departure down the river	25
Difficulties of navigation	25, 26
Arrival at Wheeling	26
Flocks of wild turkeys	26
Arrival at Marietta	27
Limestone and Columbia	27
Arrival at Cincinnati	27
General Harmar's hospitality	27, 28
Captain Kirby *vs.* Captain Kersey	28, 29
General Jonathan Forman noticed	29
General Harmar's defeat	30
Indian rendezvous at Scioto	30
Gallipolis settlement	30, 31
Anecdote of Captain Osmun	31
Arrival at Louisville	32
Fort Jefferson; Fort Steuben	32
Ensign Luce and North Bend	32, 33
Lacassangue and his station	33, 34
Early dancing parties at Louisville	35, 36
Generals Wilkinson and St. Clair	35
Dr. John F. Carmichael	36
Ezekiel Forman starts for Natchez	36
Effort to lure ashore and destroy Forman's party	37
Louisville incidents; Ashby and family; Mr. Smith; mocassins at balls	38, 39
An egg-nog frolic	39, 40
The Sabbath kept by S. S. Forman	40
A billiard-table at Louisville	40, 41
A fleet of tobacco boats	41
Mr. Buckner purchases Mr. Forman's goods	42
Mr. Forman's mishap	42
Departure from Louisville	42, 43
Incident at Fort Massac	43
Planters and sawyers	44
Mouth of the Ohio	44, 45

An Indian alarm.. 45
Indian visit; dinner... 46
Visit Indian village... 46, 47
Arrival at *L'Anse a la Graisse*................................ 47
Lieutenant Foucher's hospitality................................ 48–50
Lieutenant Foucher noticed...................................... 47, 48–50
Colonel Pope's tour cited....................................... 50
Colonel P. B. Bruin noticed..................................... 51, 52
A cub bear.. 52
Arrival at Natchez.. 52
Walnut Hills settlement project................................. 52, 53
Dr. O'Fallon; General Clark; Colonel Holder.................... 52, 53
Natchez and surroundings.. 53
Sir Wm. Dunbar noticed.. 54
S. S. Forman's land grant....................................... 55, 58, 59
Fine society at Natchez... 56
Mons. and Madame Mansant.. 56
Major Stephen Minor noticed..................................... 56, 57
Colonel Anthony Hutchins noticed................................ 56
Sickly at Natchez in 1790....................................... 56, 57
A round of visits... 57, 58
Bad treatment of servants....................................... 59
Colonel Osmun noticed... 59, 60
Departure for New Orleans....................................... 60
A genial priest... 60, 61
Voyage and incidents to Philadelphia............................ 61–63

www.ingramcontent.com/pod-product-compliance
Lightning Source LLC
Chambersburg PA
CBHW020248090426
42735CB00010B/1863